SURF*less* LAW

Introduction

SURF*less* has spent countless hours researching the Internet in order to identify, organize, and provide only the world's leading sites. SURF*less* scours the web for user-friendly sites which are rich with valuable information. No sites have paid to be listed! In addition to top quality sites, this guide is also filled with valuable tips which will improve your research skills and speed. No more browsing through endless search results and irrelevant sites. SURF*less* will get you where you want to be -- quickly and easily.

How to Use this Guide

Each page of this guide follows the same basic format. The column to the left lists web site names. The column to its immediate right, with blue text, contains the Internet addresses. The column on the far right, under the word Notes, is provided for you to record passwords, comments, and evaluations of each site. A typical site entry is provided below.

Site Name	Web Site Address	Notes
SurfLess	www.surfless.com	*Easy to navigate, fast loading. Great for gifts!*

Remember, SURF*less*, Find More!

TABLE OF CONTENTS

This research guide contains information on a variety of topics. Please note that sites in the General Internet Resources area are invaluable tools which may be used to find information on ANY subject as well as new Law sources as they become available in the future.

Best of Tips

★ Use your browser's "Open in New Window" command to utilize several browser windows at once. This will GREATLY increase your researching speed. To use this feature simply place the cursor over the site you would like to visit, then click on the right mouse button and select "Open in New Window." Using this command will NOT close the window from which you selected the next site but will minimize it. To move between open/minimized windows, click on the rectangular boxes located on the taskbar, which lies at the bottom of your screen.

★ When a page does not load try to move "up" a level by deleting everything to the right of the last "/" symbol in the URL address window. Keep trying this until the page will load. For example www.broadcast.com/personalinterests/cooking will not load. Try www.broadcast.com/personalinterests/. If this does not load, try www.broadcast.com

★ Remember while surfing the Internet to take notes in this SurfLess guidebook to quickly and easily navigate back to the Internet sites you like best.

★ Internet search engines and directory sites use different methods to scour the net for information. To ensure that you are not missing valuable information be sure to type your query into multiple engines and directory sites. See General Search Sites on page i!

★ If a web site does not appear on the first try, check the address spelling and capitalization and try again. Sites often experience technical difficulties making them temporarily unavailable.

★ Use your browser's "find in page" or "find in frame" commands to locate words within text intensive sites. In Netscape Navigator 4.x & Internet Explorer 5.x go to Edit then select "Find in Page."

General Law

Mega Law Sites

AllLaw	www.alllaw.com
ABA Researching	www.abanet.org/lawlink/home.html
American Law Sources Online	www.lawsource.com/also
CataLaw	www.catalaw.com
Cornell Legal Info. Institute	www.law.cornell.edu
Counsel Quest	www.counselquest.com
Courts.net	www.courts.net
Emory Law Library	www.law.emory.edu/LAW/refdesk/toc.html
FastSearch: The Law Engine!	www.fastsearch.com/law/main.htm
Findlaw	www.findlaw.com
GSU Law MetaIndex	gsulaw.gsu.edu/metaindex
Hieros Gamos	www.hg.org
ILRG	www.ilrg.com
Internet Law Library	law.house.gov/1.htm
Jurist Legal Education Network	jurist.law.pitt.edu

Law.com	www.law.com
Law Forum	www.lawforum.net
Law Guru	www.lawguru.com
LawInfo.com	www.lawinfo.com
Law Library of Congress	lcweb2.loc.gov/glin/worldlaw.html
Law Libr. Resource Exchange	www.llrx.com
Law Research	www.lawresearch.com
Piper Resources	www.piperinfo.com/state/states.html
Rominger Legal	www.romingerlegal.com
The Virtual Chase	www.virtualchase.com
Washburn U. School of Law	www.washlaw.edu
WWW Virtual Law Library	www.law.indiana.edu/v-lib
Yahoo Legal Resources	dir.yahoo.com/Government/Law
Yale Law School: Avalon	www.yale.edu/lawweb/avalon/avalon.htm

★   Web addresses are case sensitive.

★   When searching for a company or entity try to use www.entityname.com. For example: www.ford.com.

Legal News

CourtTV	www.courttv.com
FindLaw Legal News	www.legalnews.findlaw.com
Jurist	jurist.law.pitt.edu
Law News Network	www.lawnewsnetwork.com
Law Street Journal	www.lawstreet.com/journal
Law Techonology News	www.ljx.com/ltpn
LawMoney.com	www.lawmoney.com
Legal News Network	www.legalnewsnet.com
QuickLaw America: Legal News	www.currentlegal.com/LegalNews
The Lawyer Online (UK)	www.the-lawyer.co.uk
The New York Law Journal	www.nylj.com

Client/Consumer Focused Sites

Americounsel	expertpages.com
DesktopLawyer (UK)	www.desktoplawyer.net
FreeAdvice.com	www.freeadvice.com
Law Street	www.lawstreet.com
Law.com	www.law.com/public
Lawoffice.com	www.lawoffice.com

Lawyers.com	www.lawyers.com
Nolo.com	www.nolo.com
TheLaw.com	www.thelaw.com
USLaw	www.uslaw.com

Finding Experts

Expert Witness Network	www.witness.net
Expert Pages	expertpages.com
Experts.com	www.experts.com
Findlaw Experts	www.findlaw.com/13experts/witness.html
Hieros Gamos: Experts	www.hg.org/ex_sel.html
National Dir. Of Expert Witnesses	www.claims.com/online.html

Finding Firms/Attorneys

Findlaw Index	www.findlaw.com/14firms/directories.html
Martindale Hubbel	www.martindale.com/locator
West's Legal Directory	www.wld.com

★ Remember while surfing the Internet to take notes in this SURF*les* guidebook to quickly and easily navigate back to the Internet sites you like best.

Legal Employment

AttorneyJobs.com	www.attorneyjobs.com	
CareerBuilder.com	www.careerbuilder.com	
Emplawyernet	www.emplawyernet.com	
Law Jobs	www.lawjobs.com	
Law-jobs.net	www.law-jobs.net	
Monster.com	www.monster.com	
NationJob Network: Legal	www.nationjob.com/legal	

Fee Based Legal Tools

BNA [Bureau of National Affairs, Inc.] www.bna.com	BNA is a leading publisher of electronic news and information on developments in law, health care, business, economics and other public policy and regulatory areas.
CaseCentral www.casecentral.com	A complete, Internet-based document hosting and litigation management system designed to give legal teams the ability to store, search, and share case-related documents.
CertifiedMail.com www.certifiedmail.com	Provides secure message delivery and tracking through your web browser. You can quickly and securely send confidential messages, and you will have proof of when they were opened.
Courtlink www.courtlink.com	Combine federal and state search results on one report and obtain case summaries, names, dockets, judgments, creditors and charges.

Cyber Secretaries www.youdictate.com	A 24-hour voice to document service. Full service dictation transcription available anywhere in the world to anyone with a telephone and an e-mail address.
Docutouch www.docutouch.com	Store, collaborate on, and digitally sign any document or file without ever having to leave your PC.
GovernNet www.govaffs.com	A system that identifies and tracks the bills that you select, and tells you when they change.
JurisDictionUSA.net www.jdusa.net	Case management, secure document publication, repository and archival, time and billing, secure e-mail, calendaring, secure client and court communication and legal news.
Law Research www.lawresearch.com	A commercial version of their free link list that contains over 200,000 legal resource links worldwide.
Lexis/Nexis www.lexis-nexis.com	One of the world's largest providers of credible, in depth information.
LiveNote www.livenote.com	LiveNote enables attorneys to view, mark, annotate, search text and generate reports while on-line to the reporter as well as off-line anytime, anyplace.
Loislaw www.loislaw.com	Its state libraries contain case law, statutes, administrative codes, court rules, jury instructions, attorney general opinions, and more.

Fee Based Legal Tools continued on next page

Oliver's Cases www.oliverscases.com	Customized online delivery of federal and state appellate court opinions.
Quicklaw America, Inc. www.currentlegal.com	A full suite of primary materials including custom products that allow customers to determine what combination of laws, rules and regulations they need.
Versus www.versuslaw.com	Searchable state & federal appellate decisions.
Westlaw www.westlaw.com	Access billions of pages of information on over 13,000 Westlaw databases.
ZixMail www.zixmail.com	Enables you to communicate via encrypted and digitally signed messages with anyone in the world who has an e-mail address.

★ Use your browser's "Open in New Window" command to utilize several browser windows at once. This will GREATLY increase your researching speed. To use this feature simply place the cursor over the site you would like to visit, then click on the right mouse button and select "Open in New Window." Using this command will NOT close the window from which you selected the next site but will minimize it. To move between open/minimized windows, click on the rectangular boxes located on the taskbar, which lies at the bottom of your screen.

★ When a page does not load, try to move "up" a level by deleting everything to the right of the last "/" symbol in the URL address window. Keep trying this until the page will load. For example, www.law.com/topic/contracts will not load. Try www.law.com/topic/. If this does not load, try www.law.com.

★ Check a site's privacy policy before supplying personal information. Does the site have a policy against selling the information to marketers?

Writing Aids

DICTIONARIES/ENCYCLOPEDIAS		Notes
Columbia Encyclopedia	www.bartleby.com/65	
Dictionary.com	www.dictionary.com	
Duhaim's Law Dictionary	wwlia.org:80/diction.htm	
LawOffice.com Legal Tools	www.lawoffice.com/tools/lawtools.htm	
Nolo's Law Dictionary	www.nolo.com/dictionary/wordindex.cfm	
Nolo's Legal Encyclopedia	www.nolo.com/briefs.html	
OneLook Dictionary	www.onelook.com	
Oran's Law Dictionary	www.lawoffice.com/pathfind/orans/orans.asp	
Wordsmyth Dictionary & Thesaurus	www.lightlink.com/bobp/wedt	
OTHER AIDS		
Bartleby.com Great Books	www.bartleby.com	
Basic Legal Citation (BlueBook)	www.law.cornell.edu/citation/citation.table.html	
Columbia Guide to Online Citation	www.columbia.edu/cu/cup/cgos	
Familiar Quotations	www.columbia.edu/acis/bartleby/bartlett	
Online English Grammar	www.edunet.com/english/grammar/index.html	
Grammer Slammer	englishplus.com/grammar	
Roget's Thesaurus	humanities.uchicago.edu/forms_unrest/ROGET.html	
Shepard's	www.bender.com	
Strunk: Elements of Style	www.bartleby.com/141	

Federal Law Resources

Federal Law/Rules

Code of Federal Regulations (CFR)	www.access.gpo.gov/nara/cfr/index.html
Federal Register (FR)	www.gpo.ucop.edu/search/default.html
Rules of Appellate Procedure	www.dcd.uscourts.gov/frap-index.html
Rules of Civil Procedure	www.law.cornell.edu/rules/frcp
Rules of Criminal Procedure	www.dcd.uscourts.gov/frcrp-index.html
Rules of Evidence	www.law.cornell.edu/rules/fre
U.S. Code	www.gpo.ucop.edu:80/search/uscode.html OR www.law.cornell.edu/uscode
U.S. Constitution	www.law.cornell.edu:80/constitution/constitution.overview.html

Selected Federal Government Sites

Dept. of Commerce	www.doc.gov	Food & Drug Administration	www.fda.gov
Dept. of Energy	www.doe.gov	Internal Revenue Service (IRS)	www.irs.gov
Dept. of Health/Human Svcs	www.os.dhhs.gov	Library of Congress	lcWeb.loc.gov
Dept. of Justice	www.usdoj.gov	Natl. Archives & Records Admin.	www.nara.gov
Dept. of Labor	www.dol.gov	Natl. Labor Relations Brd (NLRB)	www.nlrb.gov
Dept. of Transportation	www.dot.gov	Sec. and Exchange Commission(SEC)	www.sec.gov
Env. Protection Agency	www.epa.gov	U.S. Copyright Office	lcweb.loc.gov/copyright
Fed. Comm. Commission	www.fcc.gov	U.S. Patent and Trademark Office	www.uspto.gov
Fed. Mediation & Conciliation Srvs	www.fmcs.gov	U.S. Census Bureau	www.census.gov
Federal Trade Commission	www.ftc.gov	White House	www.whitehouse.gov

Federal Information Gateways

All Law: Federal Info.	www.alllaw.com/law/federal_law/
ALSO: Federal Gov.	www.lawsource.com/also/usa.cgi?us1
Emory Law: U.S. Gov.	www.law.emory.edu/LAW/refdesk/country/us/fedag.html
Fed. Gov. Info. Exchange: A-Z	www.info.gov/fed_directory/list_a-d.shtml
Federal Web Locator	www.infoctr.edu/fwl
FedLaw	www.legal.gsa.gov
FedWorld.gov	www.fedworld.gov
Gov. Printing Office	www.gpo.gov
Library of Congress Internet	lcweb.loc.gov/global/explore.html
LSU: U.S. Fed. Gov. Agencies Dir.	www.lib.lsu.edu/gov/fedgov.html
VLL: U.S. Government	www.law.indiana.edu/v-lib

★ Search engines and directories are not the same. Directories are lists of web pages that are compiled by humans and organized into categories and sub-categories. Search engines are computer programs that find web pages by hunting for key words or phrases in titles, descriptions and text of pages.

★ If your Internet connection is intolerably slow, try turning off the graphics features of your Internet browser. See your browser's help for detailed instructions.

Federal Courts with Opinions

Index	www.ll.georgetown.edu/Fed-Ct OR www.findlaw.com/casecode/courts
Sup. Ct.	supct.law.cornell.edu/supct OR www.ll.georgetown.edu:80/Fed-Ct/supreme.html
1st Cir.	www.law.emory.edu/1circuit
2nd Cir.	www.law.pace.edu/lawlib/legal/us-legal/judiciary/second-circuit.html
3rd Cir.	vls.law.vill.edu/Locator/3/index.htm
4th Cir.	www.law.emory.edu/4circuit
5th Cir.	www.law.utexas.edu/us5th
6th Cir.	www.law.emory.edu/6circuit
7th Cir.	www.kentlaw.edu/7circuit
8th Cir.	ls.wustl.edu/8th.cir
9th Cir.	vls.law.vill.edu/Locator/9/index.htm
10th Cir.	www.kscourts.org/ca10
11th Cir.	www.law.emory.edu/11circuit
D.C. Cir.	www.cadc.uscourts.gov
Fed. Cir.	www.ll.georgetown.edu/Fed-Ct/cafed.html

State Law Resources

Mega Law Sites- State Indices

American Law Sources Online	www.lawsource.com/also
FindLaw	www.findlaw.com/11stategov/index.html
Hieros Gamos	www.hg.org/usstates.html
Internet Law Library	law.house.gov/17.htm
Internet Legal Resource Guide	www.ilrg.com/gov.html
Law.com	law.com/loclinks.asp?K=980
Law Research	www.lawresearch.com/v2/cstate7.htm
Legal Forms	www.uslegalforms.com/free.htm
Legal Information Institute	www.law.cornell.edu/states/listing.html
Municipal Code Corporation	www.municode.com/database.html
Municipal Codes Online	www.spl.org/govpubs/municode.html
National Center for State Courts	www.ncsc.dni.us/court/sites/courts.htm
Piper Resources	www.piperinfo.com/state/states.html
Rominger Legal	www.romingerlegal.com/states.htm
Washburn U. School of Law	www.washlaw.edu

★   Use quotation marks to search for exact phrases in search engines.

★   To learn more about Internet search engines go to www.searchenginewatch.com.

State	Home Page	Legislative Home	Judicial Home
AK	www.state.ak.us	www.legis.state.ak.us	www.alaska.net/~akctlib/homepage.htm
AL	www.state.al.us	www.legislature.state.al.us	www.alalinc.net/system.htm
AR	www.state.ar.us	www.arkleg.state.ar.us	courts.state.ar.us
AZ	www.state.az.us	www.azleg.state.az.us	www.supreme.state.az.us/welcome.htm
CA	www.state.ca.us	www.assembly.ca.gov	www.courtinfo.ca.gov
CO	www.state.co.us	w^3.state.co.us/gov_dir/stateleg.html	www.courts.state.co.us/sitemap.htm
CT	www.state.ct.us	www.cga.state.ct.us	www.jud.state.ct.us
DE	www.state.de.us	w^3.state.de.us/research/assembly.htm	www.lawlib.widener.edu/pages/deopind.htm
FL	www.state.fl.us	www.leg.state.fl.us	www.flcourts.org
GA	www.state.ga.us	www.state.ga.us/legis	www.doas.state.ga.us/courts/supreme
HI	www.state.hi.us	telnet://fyi.uhcc.hawaii.edu	www.hawaii.gov/jud/index.html
IA	www.state.ia.us	www.legis.state.ia.us	www.judicial.state.ia.us
ID	www.state.id.us	w^3.state.id.us/legislat/legislat.html	www.state.id.us/judicial/judicial.html
IL	www.state.il.us	www.legis.state.il.us	www.state.il.us/court
IN	www.state.in.us	www.state.in.us/legislative	www.state.in.us/judiciary
KS	www.state.ks.us	www.state.ks.us/public/legislative	w^3.law.ukans.edu/kscourts/kscourts.html

NOTE: w^3 = www - NOTE: w^3 = www - NOTE: w^3 = www - NOTE: w^3 = www - NOTE: w^3 = www

KY	www.state.ky.us	www.lrc.state.ky.us/home.htm	www.aoc.state.ky.us/intro.htm
LA	www.state.la.us	www.legis.state.la.us	www.state.la.us/state/judicial.htm
MA	www.state.ma.us	www.state.ma.us/legis/legis.htm	www.state.ma.us/courts/courts.htm
MD	www.state.md.us	mlis.state.md.us	www.courts.state.md.us
ME	www.state.me.us	w^3.state.me.us/legis/homepage.htm	www.courts.state.me.us
MI	www.state.mi.us	www.michiganlegislature.org	www.migov.state.mi.us/governmentBranches_Judicial.shtm
MN	www.state.mn.us	www.leg.state.mn.us	www.courts.state.mn.us/index.html
MO	www.state.mo.us	www.moga.state.mo.us	www.osca.state.mo.us
MS	www.state.ms.us	www.ls.state.ms.us	www.mssc.state.ms.us/default.asp
MT	www.state.mt.us	leg.state.mt.us	www.lawlibrary.state.mt.us/mtlegal.htm
NC	www.state.nc.us	www.ncga.state.nc.us/index.shtml	www.aoc.state.nc.us
ND	www.state.nd.us	www.state.nd.us/lr	www.court.state.nd.us
NE	www.state.ne.us	w^3.unicam.state.ne.us/index.htm	www.court.nol.org
NH	www.state.nh.us	w^3.state.nh.us/gencourt/gencourt.htm	www.state.nh.us/courts/home.htm
NJ	www.state.nj.us	www.njleg.state.nj.us	www.judiciary.state.nj.us
NM	www.state.nm.us	legis.state.nm.us	www.nmcourts.com/disclaim.htm
NV	www.state.nv.us	www.leg.state.nv.us	www.leg.state.nv.us/law1.htm

NOTE: w^3 = www - NOTE: w^3 = www - NOTE: w^3 = www - NOTE: w^3 = www - NOTE: w^3 = www

14

NY	www.state.ny.us	gopher://leginfo.lbdc.state.ny.us	ucs.ljx.com
OH	www.state.oh.us	www.ohio.gov/ohio/legislat.htm	www.sconet.state.oh.us/navigat.htm
OK	www.state.ok.us	www.lsb.state.ok.us	www.oscn.net
OR	www.state.or.us	www.leg.state.or.us	159.121.112.45
PA	www.state.pa.us	www.legis.state.pa.us	www.courts.state.pa.us
RI	www.state.ri.us	w^3.state.ri.us/submenus/leglink.htm	www.ribar.com/Courts/courts.html
SC	www.state.sc.us	www.scstatehouse.net	www.state.sc.us/judicial
SD	www.state.sd.us	w^3.state.sd.us/state/legis/lrc.htm	www.state.sd.us/state/judicial
TN	www.state.tn.us	www.legislature.state.tn.us	tscaoc.tsc.state.tn.us
TX	www.state.tx.us	www.capitol.state.tx.us	www.courts.state.tx.us
UT	www.state.ut.us	www.le.state.ut.us	courtlink.utcourts.gov/opinions
VA	www.state.va.us	legis.state.va.us/vaonline/v.htm	www.courts.state.va.us/main.htm
VT	www.state.vt.us	www.leg.state.vt.us	www.state.vt.us/courts
WA	www.state.wa.us	w^3.leg.wa.gov/wsladm/default.htm	www.courts.wa.gov
WI	www.state.wi.us	www.legis.state.wi.us	www.courts.state.wi.us
WV	www.state.wv.us	www.legis.state.wv.us/legishp.html	www.state.wv.us/wvsca
WY	www.state.wy.us	legisweb.state.wy.us	courts.state.wy.us

NOTE: w^3 = www - NOTE: w^3 = www - NOTE: w^3 = www - NOTE: w^3 = www - NOTE: w^3 = www

State Bars

AK	www.alaskabar.org	**KY**	www.kybar.org	**NY**	www.nysba.org
AL	www.alabar.org	**LA**	www.lsba.org	**OH**	www.ohiobar.org
AR	www.arkbar.com	**MA**	www.massbar.org	**OK**	www.okbar.org
AZ	www.azbar.org	**MD**	www.msba.org	**OR**	www.osbar.org
CA	www.calbar.org	**ME**	www.mainebar.org	**PA**	www.pabar.org
CO	www.cobar.org	**MI**	www.michbar.org	**RI**	ribar.com
CT	www.ctbar.org	**MN**	www.mnbar.org	**SC**	www.scbar.org
DC	www.dcbar.org	**MO**	www.mobar.org	**SD**	www.sdbar.org
DE	www.dsba.org	**MS**	www.msbar.org	**TN**	www.tba.org
FL	www.flabar.org	**MT**	www.montanabar.org	**TX**	www.texasbar.com
GA	www.gabar.org	**NC**	www.ncbar.org	**UT**	www.utahbar.org
HI	www.hsba.org	**ND**		**VA**	www.vsb.org
IA	www.iowabar.org	**NE**	www.nebar.com	**VT**	www.vtbar.org
ID	www.state.id.us/isb	**NH**	www.nhbar.org	**WA**	www.wsba.org
IL	www.illinoisbar.org	**NJ**	www.njsba.com	**WI**	www.wisbar.org
IN	www.ai.org/isba	**NM**	www.nmbar.org	**WV**	www.wvbar.org
KS	www.ksbar.org	**NV**	www.nvbar.org	**WY**	www.wyomingbar.org

Association of Trial Lawyers of America - www.atlanet.com

AK		KY	www.kata.org	NY	www.nystla.org
AL	www.atla.net	LA	www.ltla.org	OH	www.oatlaw.org
AR	www.arktla.org	MA		OK	www.otla.org
AZ	www.aztla.or	MD		OR	www.otla-online.org
CA	www.caoc.com	ME	www.mtla.org	PA	www.pabar.org
CO	www.ctlanet.org	MI		RI	
CT	www.ct-tla.org	MN	www.mntla.com	SC	www.sctla.org
DC		MO	www.matanet.org	SD	
DE	www.dtla.org	MS		TN	
FL	www.aftl.org	MT	www.monttla.com	TX	www.ttla.com
GA	www.gtla.org	NC	www.ncatl.org	UT	www.utla.org
HI	www.clh.org	ND		VA	www.vtla.com
IA	www.itla.org	NE	www.nebraskatrial.com	VT	www.vtla.org
ID		NH	www.nhtla.org	WA	www.wstla.org
IL	www.iltla.com	NJ		WI	www.watl.org
IN	www.i-t-l-a.org	NM		WV	www.wvtla.org
KS	www.ink.org/public/ktla	NV	www.ntla.org	WY	www.tcd.net\~wtla

Law by Practice Area

Mega Law Sites- Area Indices

American Law Sources Online	www.lawsource.com/also/usa.cgi?us3#X3Q
American Bar Association	www.abanet.org/sections.html
CataLaw	www.catalaw.com/info/map.shtml#Topic
Emory Law Library Reference Desk	www.law.emory.edu/LAW/refdesk/subject
FindLaw	www.findlaw.com/01topics/index.html
Hieros Gamos	www.hg.org/hg2.html
Internet Legal Resource Guide	www.ilrg.com/subject_ref.html
Law Research	www.lawresearch.com/v2/ctindex8.htm
Legal Information Institute	www.law.cornell.edu/topics/topic1.html (Alphabetical)
	www.law.cornell.edu/topics/topic2.html (Categorized)
Washburn U. School of Law	www.washlaw.edu/subject/subject.html
WWW Virtual Law Library	www.law.indiana.edu/v-lib

★ If you can not find an area listed in the following table try the more extensive lists which are available at the MegaLaw Area Indices provided above.

★ Use the following area specific sites to lead you to other sites available in your area.

Area Specific Materials

ADMINISTRATIVE LAW

ABA Admin. and Reg. Section	www.abanet.org/adminlaw/home.html
ABA Admin. Proc. Database	www.law.fsu.edu/library/admin
CataLaw Administrative	www.catalaw.com/topics/Administrative.shtml
FindLaw Administrative Law	www.findlaw.com/01topics/00administrative
Heiros Gamos Admin. Law	www.hg.org/adm.html
LII Admin. Law Materials	www.law.cornell.edu/topics/administrative.html
Nat. Assoc. of Sec. of State: Rules	www.nass.org/acr/acrdir.htm
Regulation.org	www.regulation.org
Virtual Law Library Admin. Law	www.law.indiana.edu/v-lib

ALTERNATIVE DISPUTE RESOLUTION

ADR & Mediation Resources	adrr.com
American Arbitration Assoc.	www.adr.org
CataLaw ADR	www.catalaw.com/topics/ADR.shtml
Creative Response to Conflict	members.aol.com/Altdisres/ADR.html
FindLaw ADR	www.findlaw.com/01topics/11disputeres

Hieros Gamos ADR	www.hg.org/adr.html
LII ADR	www.law.cornell.edu/topics/adr.html
Mediation Info. and Resource Center	www.mediate.com/resolution.cfm
U.S. Dept. of Labor ADR	www.dol.gov/dol/asp/public/programs/adr/main.htm

ANTITRUST

ABA Antitrust Division	www.abanet.org/antitrust/home.html
American Antitrust Institute	www.antitrustinstitute.org
Antitrust Policy Page	www.antitrust.org
Antitrust Case Summary Browser	www.stolaf.edu/people/becker/antitrust/antitrust.html
Antitrust Law & Econ. Review	webpages.metrolink.net/~cmueller
CataLaw ADR	www.catalaw.com/topics/ADR.shtml
Competition Online	www.clubi.ie/competition/compframesite
DOJ Antitrust Division	www.usdoj.gov/atr/index.html
Emory Law Securities & Antitrust	www.law.emory.edu/LAW/refdesk/subject/sec.html
Federal Trade Commission	www.ftc.gov
FindLaw Antitrust Law	www.findlaw.com/01topics/01antitrust
LII Antitrust Law Materials	www.law.cornell.edu/topics/antitrust.html

BANKRUPTCY

American Bankruptcy Institute	www.abiworld.org
Bankruptcy Online	www.fedfil.com/bankruptcy
CataLaw Bankruptcy	www.catalaw.com/topics/Bankruptcy.shtml
Emory Law Bankruptcy	www.law.emory.edu/LAW/refdesk/subject/bank.html
FindLaw Bankruptcy Law	www.findlaw.com/01topics/03bankruptcy
Hieros Gamos Bankruptcy Law	www.hg.org/bankrpt.html
Internet Bankruptcy Library	bankrupt.com
LII Bankruptcy Law Materials	www.law.cornell.edu/topics/bankruptcy.html
Nat. Assoc. Consumer Bankruptcy Attorneys	www.nacba.com
The Bankruptcy Lawfinder	www.agin.com/lawfind

COMMUNICATIONS

ACA Center for Comm. Law	www.americancomm.org/~aca/american.htm
CataLaw Communications	www.catalaw.com/topics/Communications.shtml
Federal Comm. Law Journal	www.law.indiana.edu/fclj/pubs/pubs.html
Fed. Communications Commission	www.fcc.gov

FindLaw Communications Law	www.findlaw.com/01topics/05communications
Hieros Gamos Comm. Law	www.hg.org/communi.html
Internet Telecom Info. Resources	china.si.umich.edu/telecom
LII Communications Law Materials	www.law.cornell.edu/topics/communications.html

CONSTITUTIONAL

CataLaw Constitutional	www.catalaw.com/topics/Constitutional.shtml
Constitution Finder	www.richmond.edu/~jpjones/confinder
Emory Law Constitutional	www.law.emory.edu/LAW/refdesk/subject/const.html
FindLaw Constitutional Law	www.findlaw.com/01topics/06constitutional/index.html
Hieros Gamos Constitutional Law	www.hg.org/conlaw.html
Internat'l Constitutional Law Index	www.uni-wuerzburg.de/law/index.html
LII Constitutional Law Materials	www.law.cornell.edu/topics/constitutional.html
VLL Constitutional Law	www.law.indiana.edu/v-lib/
U.S. Constitution: Analysis	www.access.gpo.gov/congress/senate/constitution/toc.html

CONTRACTS

CataLaw Contracts	www.catalaw.com/topics/Contract.shtml
Center for Research on Contracts	crcse.business.pitt.edu

FindLaw Contract Law	www.findlaw.com/01topics/07contracts
Hieros Gamos Contract Law	www.hg.org/commerc.html
LII Contracts Law Materials	www.law.cornell.edu/topics/contracts.html
Uniform Commercial Code	www.law.cornell.edu/ucc/ucc.table.html
VLL Contracts Law	www.law.indiana.edu/v-lib

CORPORATE/BUSINESS

Companiesonline.com	www.companiesonline.com
Company Sleuth	www.companysleuth.com
Delaware Corp. Law Clearinghouse	www.corporate-law.widener.edu
FindLaw Corporate Law	www.findlaw.com/01topics/08corp
Hieros Gamos Corporate Law	www.hg.org/corp.html
Hoover's Online	www.hoovers.com
LII Corporations Materials	www.law.cornell.edu/topics/corporations.html
SEC	www.sec.gov
SEC Edgar Database	www.sec.gov/edgarhp.htm
SECLaw.Com	www.seclaw.com
VLL Business & Commercial	www.law.indiana.edu/v-lib

CRIMINAL

ACLU Criminal Justice Index	www.aclu.org/issues/criminal/ircj.html
CataLaw Criminal	w.catalaw.com/topics/Criminal.shtml
CopNet	police.sas.ab.ca
Emory Law Criminal Law	www.law.emory.edu/LAW/refdesk/subject/crim.html
FindLaw Criminal Law	www.findlaw.com/01topics/09criminal
Hieros Gamos Criminal Law	www.hg.org/crime.html
Justice Information Center	ncjrs.aspensys.com
LII Criminal Law Materials	www.law.cornell.edu/topics/criminal.html
Nat.Archive of Criminal Justice Data	www.icpsr.umich.edu/NACJD/home.html
VLL Criminal Law	www.law.indiana.edu/v-lib

ENVIRONMENTAL

ABA Nat. Resources/Environmental	www.abanet.org/sonreel/home.html
CataLaw Environmental Law	www.catalaw.com/topics/Environment.shtml
Earthlaw	www.earthlaw.org
ECONet	www.igc.org/igc/econet
Emory Law Environmenal Law	www.law.emory.edu/LAW/refdesk/subject/env.html

24

Environmental Law Alliance	www.elaw.org
EPA	www.epa.gov
FindLaw Environmental Law	www.findlaw.com/01topics/13environmental
Hieros Gamos Environmental Law	www.hg.org/environ.html
LII Environmental Law Materials	www.law.cornell.edu/topics/environmental.html
VLL Environmental Law	www.law.indiana.edu/v-lib

FAMILY

ABA Comm. on Domestic Violence	www.abanet.org/domviol/home.html
ABA Family Law Section	www.abanet.org/family/home.html
Adoption Statutes, Codes and Links	www.plumsite.com/shea/states.html
Ancestry.com	www.ancestry.com
DivorceNet	www.law.cornell.edu/topics/topic2.html
DivorceSource	www.divorcesource.com
Emory Law Family Law	www.law.emory.edu/LAW/refdesk/subject/family.html
FindLaw Family Law	www.findlaw.com/01topics/15family
Hieros Gamos Family Law	www.hg.org/family.html
LII Family Law Materials	www.law.cornell.edu/topics/topic2.html#familylaw

VLL Family Law	www.law.indiana.edu/v-lib

GOVERNMENT CONTRACTS

Federal Acquisition Jumpstation	nais.nasa.gov/fedproc/home.html
FindLaw Government Contracts	www.findlaw.com/01topics/18govcontracts
GovCon	www.govcon.com
Hieros Gamos Government Law	www.hg.org/govern.html
LII Government Contracts Materials	www.law.cornell.edu/topics/government_contracts.html
The Federal Marketplace	www.fedmarket.com
U.S. Government Printing Office	www.access.gpo.gov/su_docs

HEALTH

CataLaw Health Law	www.catalaw.com/topics/Health.shtml
Center for Health Law Studies	lawlib.slu.edu/healthcenter/research/research_index.htm
FastSearch Medical Resources	www.fastsearch.com/med/index.html
FindLaw Health Law	www.findlaw.com/01topics/19health
Hieros Gamos Health Law	www.hg.org/health.html
LII Health Law Materials	www.law.cornell.edu/topics/health.html
World Health Organization	www.who.org

Amer. Imm. Lawyers Assoc.	www.aila.org
Amer. Immigration on the Internet	www.immigration-usa.com/resource.html
CataLaw Immigration	www.catalaw.com/topics/Immigration.shtml
Center for Immigration Studies	www.cis.org
DOL Immigration Collection	www.oalj.dol.gov/libina.htm
Emory Immigration Law	www.law.emory.edu/LAW/refdesk/subject/immigration.html
FindLaw Immigration Law	www.findlaw.com/01topics/20immigration/index.html
Hieros Gamos Immigration Law	www.hg.org/immig.html
Immigration Law Center	www.legalsoft.net
LII Immigration and Naturalization	www.law.cornell.edu/topics/immigration.html
Siskind's Immigration Bulletin	www.visalaw.com/bulletin.html
USINS Imm. and Naturalization	www.ins.usdoj.gov/law/index.html

INTELLECTUAL PROPERTY

ABA Intellectual Property Section	www.abanet.org/intelprop/home.html
CataLaw IP	www.catalaw.com/topics/IP.shtml
Emory IPLaw	www.law.emory.edu/LAW/refdesk/subject/intellectual.html

European Patent Office	www.european-patent-office.org
FindLaw Intellectual Property Law	www.findlaw.com/01topics/23intellectprop
FirstUse.com	www.firstuse.com
Franklin Pierce: IP Mall	www.ipmall.fplc.edu
Hieros Gamos IP Law	www.hg.org/intell.html
IP Network	www.patents.ibm.com
IP Magazine	www.ipmag.com
LII Intellectual Property Materials	www.law.cornell.edu/topics/topic2.html#intellectualproperty
Researching IP: Internat'l Context	www.llrx.com/features/iplaw.htm
STO's Patent Search System	metalab.unc.edu/patents/intropat.html
US Copyright Office	lcweb.loc.gov/copyright
US Patent & Trademark Office	www.uspto.gov
USPTO Mark & Patent Searches	www.uspto.gov/web/menu/search.html
VLL Intellectual Law	www.law.indiana.edu/v-lib

INTERNATIONAL

ABA International Law Section	www.abanet.org/intlaw/home.html
Emory International Law	www.law.emory.edu/LAW/refdesk/subject/intl.html

FindLaw International Law	www.findlaw.com/01topics/24international
Global Legal Information Network	lcweb2.loc.gov/law/GLINv1
Hieros Gamos International Law	www.hg.org/internat.html
International Court of Justice	www.icj-cij.org
LawLinks	library.ukc.ac.uk/library/netinfo/intnsubg/lawlinks.htm
LII International Law Materials	www.law.cornell.edu/topics/international.html
Law Lib. of Congress Nations	lcweb2.loc.gov/glin/x-nation.html
Northwestern: International Docs	www.library.nwu.edu/govpub/resource/internat
Tufts U. - Multilateral Conventions	fletcher.tufts.edu/library/library_index.html
United Nations: International Law	www.un.org/law
Washlaw Web: International	www.washlaw.edu/forint/forintmain.html
VLL International Law	www.law.indiana.edu/v-lib

INTERNET/COMPUTER

CataLaw Cyber Rights	www.catalaw.com/topics/Cyber-rights.shtml
Computer Crime Directory	www.officer.com/c_crimes.htm
Cyberspace Bar Association	www.cyberbar.net
Cyberspace Law Center	www.cybersquirrel.com/clc

Electronic Privacy Info. Center	www.epic.org
Phillips Nizer Internet Library	www.phillipsnizer.com/internetlib.htm
J. Marshal Center: IT and Privacy	www.jmls.edu/cyber/index.html
The Cyberlaw Encyclopedia	gahtan.com/techlaw

LABOR & EMPLOYMENT

ABA Labor and Employment	www.abanet.org/labor/home.html
AFL-CIO	www.aflcio.org/home.htm
CataLaw Labor & Employment	www.catalaw.com/topics/Labour.shtml
Department of Labor	www.dol.gov
Emory Labor & Employment	www.law.emory.edu/LAW/refdesk/subject/employ.html
FindLaw Labor Law	www.findlaw.com/01topics/27labor/index.html
Hieros Gamos Labor Law	www.hg.org/employ.html
LII Labor Law Materials	www.law.cornell.edu/topics/labor.html
VLL Labor & Employ. Law	www.law.indiana.edu/law/v-lib/labor.html

MARITIME/ADMIRALTY LAW

| Admiralty & Maritime Resources | Home.earthlink.net/~shiplaw |
| AdmiraltyLaw.com | www.admiraltylaw.com |

International Maritime Organization	www.imo.org
LII Admiralty Materials	www.law.cornell.edu/topics/admiralty.html
Maritime Global Net	www.mglobal.com
NSNet	www.nsnet.com
The Captain's Maritime Links	www.ime.net/~drwebb/maritime.html
MEDICAL MALPRACTICE RESOURCES	
AMA Doctor Finder	www.ama-assn.org/aps/amahg.htm
Emory Medical Law Resources	ww.law.emory.edu/LAW/refdesk/subject/med.html
FastSearch MedEngine	www.fastsearch.com/med/index.html
Martindale's Health Science Guide	www-sci.lib.uci.edu/~martindale/HSGuide.html
Multimedia Medical Reference Lib.	www.med-library.com/medlibrary
NIH Medline	www.nlm.nih.gov/databases/freemedl.html
OSHA	www.osha.gov
PDR.net	www.pdrnet.com
Pharmaceutical Info. Network	pharminfo.com/phrmlink.html
RX List	www.rxlist.com
Vesalius: Visual Surgery	www.vesalius.com

PROPERTY/REAL ESTATE

ABA Real Property & Probate	www.abanet.org/rppt/home.html
CataLaw Real & Personal Property	www.catalaw.com/topics/Property.shtml
Emory Law Property & Real Estate	www.law.emory.edu/LAW/refdesk/subject/prop.html
FindLaw Property Law	www.findlaw.com/01topics/33property
Hieros Gamos Property Law	www.hg.org/realest.html
LII Landlord/Tenant Materials	www.law.cornell.edu/topics/landlord_tenant.html
Land Use	www.law.cornell.edu/topics/land_use.html
Real Estate Transactions	www.law.cornell.edu/topics/real_estate.html
Property Assessments Online	www.people.virginia.edu/~dev-pros/Realestate.html
VLL Property Law	www.law.indiana.edu/v-lib

SECURITIES

10-K Wizard	www.tenkwizard.com
CataLaw Finance & Securities	www.catalaw.com/topics/Securities.shtml
Emory Law Securities & Antitrust	www.law.emory.edu/LAW/refdesk/subject/sec.html
FindLaw Securities Law	www.findlaw.com/01topics/34securities
FreeEDGAR	www.freeedgar.com
Global Securities Information, Inc.	www.gsionline.com

Hieros Gamos Securities Law	www.hg.org/security.html
Legal Forms for Corp. and Securities	www.jefren.com
SEC	www.sec.gov
SEC Edgar Database	www.sec.gov/edgarhp.htm
SECLaw.Com	www.seclaw.com
Stanford Securities Class Actions	securities.stanford.edu

TAX

ABA Tax Section	www.abanet.org/tax/home.html
CataLaw Tax Law	www.catalaw.com/topics/Tax.shtml
Emory Law Tax Law	wwww.law.emory.edu/LAW/refdesk/subject/tax.html
FindLaw Tax Law	www.findlaw.com/01topics/35tax/index.html
Hieros Gamos Tax Law	www.hg.org/tax.html
IRS	www.irs.gov
LII Tax Materials	www.law.cornell.edu/topics/topic2.html#taxation
TaxMaster.com	vls.law.vill.edu/prof/maule/taxmaster/taxhome.htm
TaxResources.com	www.taxresources.com
TaxWire	www.tax.org/TaxWire/taxwire.htm

The Tax Prophet	www.taxprophet.com
Uncle Fed.com	www.unclefed.com
VLL Tax Law	www.law.indiana.edu/v-lib

TORT

ABA Tort Section	www.abanet.org/tips/home.html
Emory Law Tort	www.law.emory.edu/LAW/refdesk/subject/tort.html
FindLaw Tort Law	www.findlaw.com/01topics/22tort/index.html
Hieros Gamos Tort Law	www.hg.org/torts.html
Internet Law Library Tort Materials	law.house.gov/110.htm
LII Tort Materials	www.law.cornell.edu/topics/torts.html
OSHA	www.osha.gov
Products Liability	www.productslaw.com
VLL Tort Law	www.law.indiana.edu/v-lib

WILLS, TRUSTS, ESTATES

ABA Real Probate & Trust Law	www.abanet.org/rppt/home.html
Ancestry.com	www.ancestry.com
CataLaw Wills, Trusts & Estates	www.catalaw.com/topics/Estates.shtml

Emory Law Trusts & Estates	www.law.emory.edu/LAW/refdesk/subject/trusts.html
FindLaw Probate, Trusts, & Estates	www.findlaw.com/01topics/31probate/index.html
Hieros Gamos Estate and Trust Law	www.hg.org/estate.html
LII Estate & Gift Tax Materials	www.law.cornell.edu/topics/estate_gift_tax.html
Wills of Famous People	www.ca-probate.com/wills.htm

★ Vary your passwords to minimize your vulnerability should someone obtain one of your passwords. To further increase your security, incorporate numbers and graphic characters (!,@,#,$,%) into your passwords.

★ In order to save time and avoid the unnecessary retyping of web addresses, we encourage you to save your most frequently visited addresses using your Internet browser's "Bookmarking" capabilities. Consult the "help" section of your browser for details.

★ Whenever you visit a web site a record of that visit is left on your computer. To remove traces of your visit you will need to: clear your history, empty your cache, and delete your cookies. See your web browser's help section for instructions on how to perform these tasks. Also, clearing traces of your visits should improve browser performance.

★ Virus = A small computer program which attaches itself to another program and then replicates itself. Most virus programs are destructive and will damage or destroy other computer programs.

★ Cookies = Small files which some web sites use to deliver and store data to your computer. Information you enter such as your e-mail address, your login name, or the pages you have visited, may be stored on your computer by the site you are visiting. This information may be accessed later when a site is revisited. If security is a concern, you may wish to turn off "cookies" on your web browser. Check your browser's help files for information on how to turn "cookies" off.

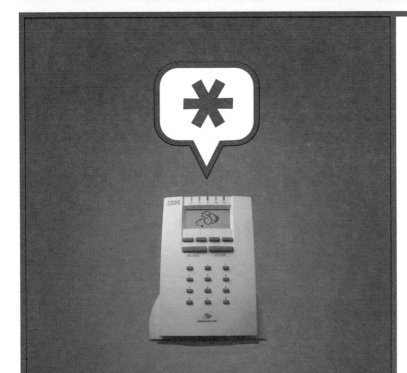

All the technology you need to build a stronger law firm, direct from IBM. In fact, we can connect everyone in your office to the Internet, help you establish Web presence and even deliver the latest award-winning hardware, software and services.

> **WebConnections for Lawyers.** In one easy-to-install package, you get e-mail for up to 100 users at yourfirm.com, 24 x 7 x human support[1], firewall security and much more. Subscriptions start at only $99 per month[2].

> **The IBM Web Starter Kit.** Now, you don't have to be a Web expert to have your own site. Starting at only $499[3], we'll design and build it for you, register your own URL, and even include six months of hosting.

> **The latest e-business tools and software.** Give your firm a competitive edge with savings on award-winning IBM hardware and software, like ThinkPad® notebooks, Netfinity® servers, IBM PCs, flat panel monitors, Lotus Smart Suite Millennium Edition,® and ViaVoice Millennium Pro™.

*Everything you need to build a more productive, efficient law firm; Web included.

 1 888 IBM 5800 Code # WC-LAW 164
www.ibm.com/smallbusiness/legal

GENERAL INTERNET RESOURCES

MetaSearch Engines

[These engines search multiple search engines from one site]

Debriefing	www.debriefing.com
DogPile	dogpile.com
Ixquick	www.ixquick.com
Mamma	mamma.com
MetaCrawler	metacrawler.com
Profusion	profusion.com
SavvySearch	savvysearch.com
The Big Hub	thebighub.com

Finding Places/Maps

CyberAtlas	www.delorme.com/cybermaps
MapBlast	www.mapblast.com
MapQuest	www.mapquest.com
Maps On Us	www.mapsonus.com
Rand McNally	www.randmcnally.com
YahooMaps	maps.yahoo.com

Search Engines/Tools

About.com	about.com
Altavista	altavista.com
Ask Jeeves	ask.com
Dmoz	dmoz.org
Excite	excite.com
FAST Search	alltheweb.com
Google	google.com
Go.com	go.com
Hotbot	hotbot.com
Looksmart	looksmart.com
Lycos	lycos.com
Netscape	netscape.com
Northernlight	northernlight.com
Snap	snap.com
Web Crawler	webcrawler.com
Yahoo	yahoo.com

Mailing/Tracking Packages

Airborne Express	www.airborne.com	Pitney Bowes	www.pitneybowes.com
DHL	www.dhl.com	Roadway Express	www.roadway.com
e-stamp	www.estamp.com	UPS	www.ups.com
Federal Express	www.fedex.com/us	US Postal Service	www.usps.com

Phone Numbers/Addresses

555-1212 Directory	www.555-1212.com
AnyWho	www.anywho.com
Four11 Telephone Directory	www.four11.com
Verizon superpages.com	superpages.com
InfoSpace	www.infospace.com/index_ppl.htm
International Dialing Codes	www.the-acr.com/codes/cntrycd.htm
Internet 800 Directory	www.inter800.com
Switchboard	www.switchboard.com
The Ultimates	www.theultimates.com
U.S. Postal Service Zip Codes	www.usps.gov/ncsc
Yahoo - People Search	people.yahoo.com
Yahoo - Yellow Pages	yp.yahoo.com

Travel Related

180096Hotel	www.180096hotel.com
Airline Phone Numbers/Web Sites	www.princeton.edu/Main/air800.html
American Express (ITN)	travel.americanexpress.com
Expedia.com	www.expedia.com
Last Minute Travel	www.lastminutetravel.com
TheTrip.com	www.thetrip.com
Travelocity Travel Agent	www.travelocity.com
Travelweb Agent	www.travelweb.com

News and Information

NETWORKS	
ABC	abcnews.go.com
C-SPAN	www.c–span.org
CBS	www.cbs.com/navbar/news.html
CNN	www.cnn.com
Fox	www.foxnews.com
MSNBC	www.msnbc.com

PUBLICATIONS	
AJR News Link - Global Newspaper Index	ajr.newslink.org/news.html
All the Worlds Newspapers	www.webwombat.com.au/intercom/newsprs
Chicago Tribune	www.chicago.tribune.com
LA Times	www.latimes.com
NY Times	www.nytimes.com
USA Today	www.usatoday.com
WallStreet Journal	www.wsj.com
Washington Post	www.washingtonpost.com
OTHER	
Associated Press News Wire	wire.ap.org
News Edge Newspage	www.newspage.com

Fee Based Information Gathering Tools

DataLand	www.dataland.com	"The Most Complete and Extensive Source of Investigative and Financial Information in the World"
InfoTek Intelligent Information	www.cdb.com/public	"[T]ools to conduct searches for locating people and verifying business information and assets."
KnowX	www.knowx.com	Public Records, Locate People, Research Businesses

National Credit Information Network	www.wdia.com/ catagory.htm	Birth & Death Records, Credit Checks, Criminal History Checks, Voter Registration Info. SSN Tracing, Real Estate/Property Records & More.
PublicData.com	www.publicdata.com	Search multiple records databases including: "Civil, Criminal, Driver's License, Federal Government databases, DMV - Tags and VIN, Professional, & Voter."
The American Information Network Inc.	www.ameri.com	SHERLOCK - "[L]ocate missing persons, lost relatives or even track dead beat spouses all using public records. I - D.M.V. - [D]o a search of DMV records by Drivers License Number or a License Plate Number in 47 States for violations and registration information."
The Electric Library	www.elibrary.com	Launch a comprehensive, simultaneous search through full-text newspapers, full-text magazines, newswires, classic books, maps, photographs, works of literature and art.
The Ultimates	www.theultimates.com	Search multiple resources like phone books, e-mail directories, and trip planners. Just type your search criteria into the first search engine and they are copied to others.

ADDITIONAL SITES

_____

_____

_____

_____

_____

_____

_____

_____

_____

_____

_____

_____